Tails of Basset Rescue

Christine Bly

DEDICATION

This book is dedicated to my husband, Jim. It was his dream to start a Rescue. He has always had an enormous amount of compassion for animals. His dedication to helping those who cannot help themselves has driven him to keep the Rescue going.

Rescue life is hard. It is self-sacrificing, but, oh! the joy it brings.

Without my husband's foresight, I may have never been fortunate enough to experience and share with him the extreme sense of completeness that Rescue brings.

INTRODUCTION

This book is more about survival than rescue. Rescue sounds like a glorious job, one that denotes some respect from those who hear about it, but rescue is not glorious. Rescue is more than taking in a dog, giving it a bath, and finding it a good home. Rescue is a matter of life and death. It is a struggle for both animal and human to overcome past experiences.

In this book, you will peer into both the hearts and souls of human and animal alike as they journey together; from abuse and neglect to a new life of value and safety. Within these pages you will see into the world of rescue. Not the glorious "pat us on the back" world of rescue, but the part no one wants to know about. The sad stories people do not want to hear—the truth.

The proceeds from this book will be used to fund future rescues.

Please enjoy *Tails of Basset Rescue.*

CONTENTS

DEDICATION iii

INTRODUCTION v

CONTENTS vii

Getting Started 1

Our Story...5

Bella 9

Buster...12

Clyde 16

Copper 19

Duke...22

Fancy..26

Freckles..30

Hamilton 34

Happy...37

Jo Jo 41

Looney 44

Luke 48

Millie 53

Milton 56

Molly and Stinky Peet 60

Pickles 65

Roscoe 68

Rosie/Pepper 71

Sammy 75

Sarah 78

Stanley 82

Stewie 85

Vinnie 88

Wesley 91

Wilbur 95

The PBF and ASTT 99

Rainbow Bridge..104

ACKNOWLEDGMENTS...106

ABOUT THE AUTHOR 106

GETTING STARTED

Like any other business, starting a rescue takes a lot of effort and a lot of hard work.

The first step is committing to many long hours and the hard work caring for the dogs, as well as properly taking care of paperwork and documentation.

The next step to starting a rescue is to apply for an ACFA (Animal Care Facility Act) License with the State Department of Agriculture. We had to wait about four months for the State Inspector to come to our home and inspect our records and facility for cleanliness before we could get this license with the

State.

Then we needed to become a corporation, registered with the Secretary of State in the State of Missouri where our facility is located. To become a corporation you need to set up bylaws, rules and regulations that your rescue and the people who belong to it or work for it will abide by. This takes some thinking and it took me many long nights to figure out what we wanted to include in our bylaws. Once we received the approval from the Secretary of State, then we applied for insurance for the rescue, and started our application for our 501c3. Once approved as a tax exempt organization (this took about six months) we started working on our Web site and finding foster homes.

It is a struggle to get through all of the paperwork, but it is a necessary task because without the steps to become tax exempt, all donations are considered personal income, and you would have to declare any income you receive for veterinarian bills as income on your personal income taxes. Also, any donations made to a rescue that is not an approved charity may not be deducted from the giver's income tax as a charitable donation. So, this helps us with our begging for funds to help the dogs.

We then needed to create all sorts of forms, such as Adoption Applications, Adoption Agreements, Intake Forms for tracking the rescue dogs, and Foster Home Applications.

Once we got the formal part of the rescue together, we started looking for help in Foster Homes and Volunteers. Our applications for foster homes are similar to our application for adoption; both applicants have to meet the same criteria.

We currently have only two foster homes, despite our continual begging. A third no longer keeps dogs for us, because has a rental home and her neighbor complained she had too many pets.

If we had more foster homes and more funds, we could take in more dogs. However, we just do not have enough money coming in to take in more dogs. We have been very fortunate in the foster homes we have, though, because they have been very supportive and have been a real boost to our rescue. One pays most of the vet bills for us that the dog she fosters incurs, and, when they have the funds, both have paid for vet bills for their fosters as donations to the rescue.

Rescue is a way of life—one that is so demanding that we have not been away from home in over fourteen years because of the dogs--we do not have anyone who would take care of them for us, even if we went away for just a few days.

All of our family members think we are crazy to have so many dogs and, unfortunately, do not support us in our decision to keep rescuing dogs. However, as I said, it is a very rewarding way of life. And we hope that the dogs that we get and help appreciate our commitment.

OUR STORY

My husband and I always had dogs when each of us was growing up. So, when we got married and had children, of course we had dogs then, too.

Since we always wanted big dogs and a big family, our first dog after we got married was a St Bernard. We got our first St Bernard from a friend who had a litter. We love the breed, but they like to be outside in the cold and I did not like to be outside in the cold. So, when one of our friends got a Basset Hound that was being given away because the people lost their home we took a liking to Bassets. After all, all they are big dogs like St Bernards, except they have long ears and short legs and they love to be inside with their people—so we decided to search for a Basset.

We found our first Basset in 1981 through a newspaper ad. She was an older puppy that no one wanted, so we took her in and named her Droopy Sue. We loved that little girl! She was the best dog ever. She was our inside dog and Tiny, our Saint, lived outside. We'd beg him to come in, and in the summer he would stay inside in the air conditioning. But in the winter, he did not want to be in the house, preferring the cold outside.

He loved his custom dog house that Jim built for him. It had insulation in the walls and floor, and under the roof; vinyl siding; a nice marlite interior; and a working window on the side so that he could not only look out the front, but also the side. It was a very nice dog house and he thoroughly enjoyed it!

When Droopy Sue left us, we were so heartbroken we vowed never to have a dog again. It was too hard to lose a loved family member like Droopy. But after a few years, we yearned to have another Basset. In 1996 we bought Peaches Louise from a Pet Store. Back then, we had no idea what a puppy mill was, nor what a rescue was. However, Peaches was our baby—spoiled rotten from the get-go. She ate our couch, arms and legs off chairs, and several remote controls, but we loved her more than we ever loved any other dog. Our children were by then grown-up and gone, so Peaches was our baby.

One day, my son called to tell us that he and his wife and the grandkids were at the mall and saw an all white Basset in a cage at the pet store. My husband, Jim, said, "Let's go see." And so we went. The poor Basset boy in the cage was curled up in a small ball. When he did uncurl, he was not all white after all. He was curled so tightly, all you could see was his white fur, but once uncoiled, he was a tri-color and quite a big boy—too big for his cage and for a pet store. We asked how old he was and the clerk said he was four months.

"We are going to have to send him to the pound," he said. "No one wants him. He has a bad leg." We asked if, instead of giving him to the pound, if we could buy him for half price. We soon were walking away from the store and the mall with Freckles in tow.

Freckles was our first rescue, even though we had no idea at the time what a rescue was. Since his was confined in that small cage at the pet store, his leg grew crooked and required orthopedic surgery. He was in casts the first few months we had him. But he as Peaches got along and were both very good dogs together.

One day, our neighbor found a Basset running down the highway and put him in her car before he got hit. When she brought him home, she asked us if we wanted him since he was a Basset and we had two already. So, we said, "Yes!" And then we had Rocky, our second rescue. Rocky was a loner and he bit us several times. But, after a while, with some dog training and a visit or two to the canine psychiatrist, he became the best trained dog we ever had.

One day Jim saw an ad in the Sunday paper: "Basset Rescue will be at the Pet store today. Come sign up to volunteer". We thought this was neat, so we went and signed up to help out. No one ever called us. The next month we saw the advertisement again and so we went to tell them we signed up, but that no one called us. They apologized said they all have full time jobs and volunteer on weekends and evenings and sometimes are slow about getting things done, but they would definitely keep us in mind. Two days later, we had our first foster Basset.

That was in 2001. From then on, the rescue owner taught us the business. In 2004, we formed Western Missouri Basset Rescue, Inc. We have had over 300 dogs come through our rescue since we started. Some have stayed with us until they passed on, but the majority of our rescues have found loving homes.

The look on people's faces when they open their hearts to share their lives with a new companion, and the wagging tails looking back at them are what keeps us going.

BELLA

I got a call from a lady in Southern Missouri who had taken a poor emaciated little girl from a horrible abuser who had the Basset girl only to produce puppies and make money. The lady had her a few weeks. The female had put a little weight; she kept her outside all the time.

"After all," she said. "Dogs do not belong in the house." I gritted my teeth as I listened to her story, looking over my shoulder at the eight rescue dogs laying on my couches and chairs. This woman could not keep Bella any longer because she was slated to fly overseas the following week for a new job.

It was an emergency. I had to take this poor baby or she be taken to the pound.

Every day our rescue gets a call similar to this one, but this was more desperate than most.

And so, Bella came to Western Missouri Basset Rescue. The poor little girl was only three years old, so badly covered in fleas and that she looked like she was black and grey.

Although Bella was kept as an outside Baby girl, she was completely housetrained. She is just like any other Basset, wanting to be inside with people and to be spoiled. But, unfortunately, this poor little three year-old has never had a chance to be happy in her short life.

After a bath and flea treatment, I discovered she was actually a red and white Basset.

Belle was so afraid of the other dogs, and she jumped when anyone tried to pet her. If only she could talk. Who knows what torture this poor girl has been through?

I finally coaxed Bella to come to me and I pulled her up onto my lap, snuggling with her as I whispered into her ear and stroked her straw-like fur. Her fur was so coarse--you could tell she had not been fed well. Her hair was thin and felt brittle. After a few minutes she finally relaxed and let me hold her talk to her, pet her, and caress her. After holding her a while, she looked around to make sure everything was okay and then she actually fell asleep on my lap, But during her sleep, she started jerking and running and yelping. I am sure she was dreaming of bad times, so I held her closer and gave her kisses.

She cracked her eyes open a little and actually wagged her tail—a broken spirit starting to heal.

BUSTER

My first contact with Buster's family was a phone call. "We want to give up or dog" the voice said on the other end of the line" We just do not have time for him."

I did not have room for another dog but asked her to email me a picture and I would see what I could do.

The picture came through my email a short time later and my heart melted. My mood went from happy to angry and then sad. There staring back at me from my computer was a Hound that needed help. Eyes full of puss, dirty hair with patches of red bloody areas all over his skin, and a deformed leg.

I knew no one else was going to help this dog he had too many problems and if they took him to the pound more than likely he would be put to sleep. This dog was crying out to me in the picture to save him. I called the woman back immediately and said," I will be right over to pick up Buster."

I drove to Blue Springs a twenty minute drive from my house and pulled up in the drive three young kids were playing in the yard and mom was holding Busters leash and dad put his bed in the trunk of my car. While the parents were busy I asked the four year old little boy "Won't you miss your doggie?" He replied "I used to love him but he got too big and now we do not love him anymore." This boy was four, Buster was four also, and I wanted to ask the boy how old will you be when your mom and dad decide they do not love you anymore but I bit my tongue. I wanted no reason for them to deny me taking Buster I wanted to get him away from that home as fast and peaceably as I could.

Buster and I were finally on our way to my house, what I would tell my husband, we had just talked over how we had too many hounds and needed to stop taking in more for a while, especially with me out of work because we just could not afford a bunch of vet bills. And here I am with a dog that needs entropian surgery to fix his eyes, something to help his skin clear up and orthopedic surgery on his bad leg. Well when I got home my husband was just pulling in the drive from work. He took one look at Buster then one look at me and said, "He is a beautiful dog I am glad you went and got him."

My husband is as big a sap as me when it comes to the Basset Hounds.

The next morning I took Buster to my veterinarian and we set up his surgery to fix his eyes for the first of next week. We had no money so I posted his story on the Drool a Basset Hound community thread and donations to help this dear animal started pouring in. We felt truly blessed. Buster and our rescue were going to be fine. We got his eyes done and started working on getting the staph infection cleared up that he had on his skin before we would tackle the orthopedic surgery for his leg.

When he walked, he lunged forward and sometimes would lose his balance and fall on his face. His leg was bent backward at his ankle and his lower leg was bent way forward. My vet contacted an orthopedic surgeon at the Missouri Veterinary clinic in Columbia to see what needed to be done. We took Buster to the University of Columbia Veterinary School and he was examined and we found out Buster needed surgery to correct his angular limb deformity. It was a costly surgery—almost $3,000 with all of the follow ups—but he came through it and is now able to walk.

Buster also had to have anal gland removal surgery a few months after his leg was on the mend because one of his anal sacks had a growth inside. Buster has had a lot of medical problems; he is our six-thousand-dollar dog so to speak.

He loves to go "bye bye". He thinks someday that I will take him back home. He yearns to be back where he came from and loved by those little children, but he is home for now—a healthier, happier boy even though he is not quite sure. I often have to sleep with my hand on him in the night sometimes he is afraid of the dark, and he is especially afraid of thunderstorms. But he is well, he is loved, and he is safe here in Rescue.

We wish we could find him a permanent home but, for now, he will be loved here.

CLYDE

Clyde had a rough life.

When he came to us, he could not move his back end. Clyde was first spotted trudging along on the side of a busy highway in the middle of a snow storm, dragging his back limbs behind him through the snow and ice. He was picked up by a trucker heading down to Texas, who called the local Basset Rescue near Oklahoma. They promptly went to pick him up and took him to the veterinarian in Oklahoma, where he was diagnosed with nerve damage in his back end.

The woman who was assigned to foster him had no way to give him constant care and since the rescue was full, she had to check around to see if another rescue would take him. She contacted us in Missouri and asked if my husband and I had room. She explained that Gladys with "4 The Hounds" Rescue would take him, but since he cannot walk she would have a hard time lifting him. He would not be able to navigate up and down her hilly area to get back and forth to the kennels.

"Sure," we said. "Our house is a ranch. We have hardly any steps here. Our Kitchen dog door is even with the patio, so there are no steps and there is a small three-inch drop from the patio to the back yard. He will be fine here."

The next day, we drove down by the Missouri/Arkansas border to pick up Clyde (he had been transported to there for us) and another dog from Ozark Mountain Basset Rescue.

The first thing we did after we got Clyde was to take him to our vet, who X-rayed him. There was no damage seen, but he might have just been bruised from the impact of a car. The vet put him on a daily dose of Rimadyl for his pain.

Now, Clyde was a grey Basset. He was so old—probably 14 or older when he came to our rescue—that his coloring was faded. He may have been old and he may not have been able to walk, but, boy, as he very loud. He had no problems letting you know when he wanted something. He sounded like a bellowing walrus in the zoo. Oh, the sounds he could make were so soulful; they cut right through you right to your heart.

After a few months of taking the pain medicine and lots of rest, Clyde started using his back legs again.

He was a good ol' boy—always friendly to every dog who came to stay with us. He showed the young ones the ropes, told them their boundaries, and kept them in line, always a grandfather-like figure in our home. Clyde always slept next to me in the bedroom. He was always aware of where I was and followed me wherever I went. He may have had nerve damage in his back end, but from the day he finally stood up, he was able to walk...and from just a few months after we got him until the day he passed away, he was such a loving sweet old man.

Clyde was with us four years before he succumbed to cancer in 2009.

We will miss his sweet nuzzling, his walrus- moaning bark, and his demands to always be near me. Such a grand old man. He was so full of emotion and wisdom for the rest of the pack.

We do not know how or why he was on the side of that busy highway, but we were so glad we were able to help this wonderful boy.

He touched our hearts like only he could do.

COPPER

Copper was about to be sent to the pound when the wife of the family called me and asked if I could take him. He was only four months old and a cute little guy. Although, there was not very much Basset in this boy; he was more of a coonhound, yet too cute to send to the pound.

Evidently Copper was bought as five weeks old baby by a college girl who thought she wanted a dog, but mistakenly thought that the dog would train himself. She was soon bored with taking care of the dog and, so, her friends who came over to visit ended up feeding him, cleaning up after him, walking him, and letting him out of the crate in which he was confined. One day, a friend could just not stand to see the poor puppy suffering. He took Copper away from his irresponsible friend.

Copper now had a home. But even though he was such a good boy and loved the child in his new home, the father-in-law who helped the couple purchase the house did not like the idea of them having a dog. They needed to get rid of Copper. If we did not take him, then he would go straight to the pound. The pound, we found out, was a kill shelter and few dogs make it out of there alive. So we took Copper in.

He was a bit rambunctious, but we had plenty of other dogs for him to play with and after a few weeks, he calmed down and began to fit right in with the others. Yes, he chewed some but, after all, he was a puppy. Since we always buy our furniture from the thrift store, we did not worry about a few chewed cushions. At our house, that was the norm.

A few months after we took Copper into rescue, a new foster home opened up. They wanted to foster Jack, but he was afraid to climb up and down the steps to their apartment. So they tried out Copper. Copper became quick friends with Ernie, their other Basset mix. Ernie was quite the celebrity; he happened to be the ten-thousandth dog to have been rescued and transported on a fairly new program bus. Because of this, he became the guest of honor at a big celebration that was held in St Louis Missouri. The fete had nationwide coverage about the transport bus.

Ernie won toys and dog food and all kinds of neat gifts that he shared with Copper and all the rest of our rescue dogs. Copper and Ernie each got one of the toys and some treats from the occasion. The foster family donated the rest to our rescue so that our dogs would have plenty of toys and treats, too.

In foster, Copper and Ernie were fed raw diets consisting of raw meat, strawberries, and other fruits. Consequently, they were very healthy dogs.

Copper eventually was adopted by Heather. Since then, he has had several health problems but Heather always takes him to the vet and gets him whatever treatment he needs. After all, he is Heather's little boy. She has three dogs now and loves every one of them dearly.

Many recent changes have happened in Copper's life. Heather moved from Missouri, taking Copper back East to live. Heather and her fiancé recently got married. She no longer feeds raw meat to her dogs. But Copper, Ernie, and their new housemate are all very well loved and spoiled. Heather emails us regularly to keep us informed of how great Copper is doing and she is always singing praises about our Western Missouri Basset Rescue. We are so happy that she contacted us to foster Copper and then decided to keep him.

He got a great home.

DUKE

Duke was a regular Hound dog, with sad, droopy eyes and long, floppy ears. He was just a beautiful boy.

He was left in a back yard when his owners moved away. The neighbor said Duke's owners both lost their jobs, and were losing everything else. So, they packed up and moved away, leaving Duke behind.

We drove over by Bonner Springs, Kansas to pick up Duke and brought him home with us.

Duke was not altered and we had no idea if he had ever had any shots when we got him.

I usually take all of my Bassets to one veterinary clinic to get their vet work done. I trust my clinic completely. They have very dedicated sincere professional staff. But the vet bills are high and, in rescue, money is always a big concern. Whenever we think we have enough to get by a few weeks, someone gets sick and it costs us hundreds of dollars to get them well. Next thing you know our surplus is gone.

We were experiencing a lack of funds at the time we got Duke. A friend talked me into taking Duke to a low cost Spay/Neuter place in Shawnee Mission, Kansas that would do all of his vet work and neutering for $65.00.

I called, made an appointment for Duke, and took him in to be neutered—feeling guilty and disloyal to my regular vet as I was driving Duke over there. The feelings continued for the next few days.

Duke came home from surgery later that night and rested well. However, the next morning he had a beet red mark across his belly. It looked odd to me, and he felt like he had a fever. So I took him back to the low cost clinic to have him see the doctor again. I thought something was wrong with him.

We waited to see the vet and when she finally came out, she seemed very irritated with me. I showed her the red mark on his belly. She said, "That's just a bruise. It will go away."

"He feels hot to me," I said. She did not even touch him.

"He is okay. He just had surgery. Do not worry about him," she assured me.

So, I took Duke back home and gave him some pain

medication and an aspirin.

Later that afternoon his tummy burst open.

I rushed him to my regular veterinarian and told them how I took him to the low cost clinic to get his vetting done just to save money. They were very understanding.

After examining Duke, they told me he had a horrible infection.

The clinic that I took him to had used cat gut to suture Duke. Many dogs are allergic to cat gut. Hence, many vets do not use it any more. However, it is cheaper than what most vets use, so that is probably why the low cost places use it.

As it turned out, Duke was one of the dogs who are allergic to cat gut. He had a fever of 106^0F and his belly was full of puss. The red mark was blood poisoning from the infection. Duke was placed on IV antibiotics, and was prepared for surgery to remove all of the sutures that had been put in his groin and replace them with the proper suture material.

I got Duke back home two days later with a drain in his side because the infection was still dripping out of his belly and a cone on his head so he would leave the drain alone. Despite this, he was already looking and acting more like his old hound dog self. After several new stitches and $600.00 later, he was beginning to be on the mend.

I called the low-cost place and told them what happened and how much it cost to fix him.

They said, "If you had brought him back here we would have taken care of him."

I told them how their vet acted and that I was not taking another chance with her "we weren't at fault" attitude. I also told them, "If I had given her another chance to take care of Duke, chances are he would probably be dead right now."

They refused to take any responsibility for Dukes condition or help with any of his subsequent bills.

Duke finally did well, but it took him about three weeks of antibiotic care to get all of the infection out of his belly.

He is now a success story. He was adopted and is now living the life of Reilly. But what a rough way to start out his new life.

Two months later the cut-rate vet place I took him to was shut down. It was all over the news that the veterinarian was showing unlicensed staff how to perform spays and neuters on dogs and cats. In fact, on the news they said most of the cats were done by the manager of the spay/neuter clinic instead of by a licensed vet.

This taught me a valuable lesson: Don't try to cut corners when it comes to vet care. You get what you pay for.

FANCY

Fancy's story comes to us from Marie Campbell, who works with a rescue for Newfoundlands in Florida but has saved Bassets, too.

I have done Newfoundland rescue for 17 years and I have seen some rough care of dogs but rarely are they starved. The abuse that occurs to the Bassets staggers me. I don't really understand it either in that the Basset, in general, is not a hard dog to care for. The breed temperaments tend to be exceptionally good, with a few exceptions. They are affectionate and adaptable.

I got my first basset five years ago. A well off client of ours adopted a tri-colored girl named Fancy. They got her from a private shelter at PetCo Adoption Days. By eight months old, Fancy had been sold twice, put into rescue, and adopted out again. I am her fifth owner, getting her when she was about 16 months old.

Our clients owned a huge ranch house on two acres of lake front property—valued at around $750,000 before the housing market bust. They had four dogs and a large pet turn-over—a Great Dane, an Australian Shepherd, and a Yorkshire Terrier. They kept the Yorkie on a screened in porch because they never house trained her. Eventually, they gave her away—THANK GOD! I fell in love with Fancy the minute I saw her! To me, she was perfect! They gave Fancy to me because they claimed she peed and pooped all over the house. I have had her now for five years and she has never peed or pooped in the house. Go figure.

Here is a funny story that my veterinarian tells about bassets. He has quite a few in his practice, as I guess they are popular with older people. He told me that when he gets a client in who has a basset that relieving him/herself in the house, he tells them, "This dog is not happy with you. See if he/she is attached to one of your family members or friends and let them try him/her out for a while."

I asked him why he would say such a thing and he said, "I have found that when bassets are not happy, they poop in your house. Inevitably, they will stop this behavior when they are happy in a new house." Is this funny or what?

Anyway, while in our clients' care, Fancy got run over by the father in his one-ton pickup truck!!! What saved her bacon was the fact that she was on loose sand and she sank into the ground when the truck went over her. She did have to have her left hip replaced, but her organs were fine.

The family knew I was in love with Fancy. I used to always carry her around like a baby when I visited them. She is small—a mere 36 pounds—40 pounds when too chubby. They called me when they got back from a spring vacation and asked me if I still wanted Fancy. I said, "Yes."

The wife said, "Come get her. I am taking off her shock collar (They have that underground shock fencing.) and putting her in the front yard."

I said, "If you don't mind me asking, why are you giving her away?"

She said, "She goes potty all over the house, and I have had it. What are you going to do with her?"

I said, "I will crate train her and house train her."

I called my mom, who was shopping at the time, and told her to go pick up Fancy.

When she got here, I put her in a big 700 Newfy crate with a comforter so that everyone could sniff her and get used to her without hurting her or threatening her—I find this is always the best way to get the gang used to a new dog. She was very depressed for three days, but on the third day she popped out of her crate like a Vegas showgirl out of a cake and never looked back!

She was very thin when I got her and her hip still had not healed after six months. She cried allot with the pain, she still limped, and the scar was raw looking. So, I took her to my vet. He said the implant was fine, but that she was ten pounds under weight at only 26 pounds and was suffering from malnutrition. Can you believe that a family that spent $3,500- on a hip replacement would not buy dog food???? I'll go you one better: they owner grocery stores and still did not bring dog food home!

After she gained ten pounds, she stopped limping, her hip completely healed, the scar grew hair, and she now runs like the wind—well as close to it as a basset gets anyway.

Their odd attention-deficit-hyperactive-disorder (ADHD) son was doing ninja kicks on the dogs and Fancy went from being Basset friendly and outgoing to fearful and crying when you picked her up. UGH!

Well, she is perfect now and very bossy as only a female Basset can be. The Newfs receive grooming against their will from her and if they do not play with her when she is in the mood, she will climb on them while they are sleeping and nibble on their lips.

I think Bassets, like Newfs, recognize one another. And the day we brought home Luke, she went crazy with excitement. I think it was good for him to have another Basset here to nap, play, and bond with.

FRECKLES

Most Basset Hounds have solid colored ears. When their ears are spotted, as I have recently found out, Basset breeders call them "broken ears".

Freckles was the third Basset we owned. My grandkids named him Freckles because he had a broken ear, the first Basset Hound I had ever seen with spots on his ears. Now, Freckles was our first dog with a broken ear, but he was not the last.

He was such a kind soul. He loved every other dog that came into our home. He acted like the daddy for every young pup—he was so proud of his children, always strutting around the young ones like a proud papa.

Sadly, though, Freckles had a difficult start in his life. His front legs grew crooked from being confined too long in a small cage in the pet store. Shortly after we got, him he needed to have surgery to break and reset his front legs so that it was no longer difficult for him to walk.

After his surgery, he slid around the grass, pushing his front end with his back legs while skimming his chest across the grass, with his two broken and casted front legs dragging along at his side. It was painful for him, and it took a long time for his legs to heal.

Freckles used to set his chin on the side of the bed whining for us to lift him up for a comfortable snooze. We gladly obliged—after all he was our baby. And it wasn't too long after the casts were removed when he was jumping up on the bed all by himself.

He was a very beautiful hound, with soft and shiny fur. He was a little taller than most; maybe his operation had something to do with the way his bones in his legs grew longer. In any event, he was a handsome boy—very regal looking with an extremely mild spirit.

As he got older, he began having seizures. It was very scary to see this magnificent hound with a demeanor almost that of someone born into royalty wrenching and uncontrollably jerking in a panic--eyes fixed, legs straight out—not responding to anything around him for five minutes until the seizure passed.

We took him to the vet, who drew and tested some blood. Freckles was just low on thyroid and once we got him on thyroid meds he was fine; no more seizures.

Later in his life he needed eye surgery. He had holes in his corneas—ulcers. He had to have the holes scraped and cleaned so that new tissue could form. He even had to wear contact lenses to keep any dirt or infection from getting into the eye. I wear glasses myself and have never owned contacts, mainly because it bugs me to put anything into my eye, but here I am helping this dog with his contacts. They had little black spots on them so I could tell if one fell out or if they were both still in when I gave his eye drops several times a day.

A few years after his eye surgery, Freckles suddenly went down in the back end. He just could not walk. I rushed him to the vet where he was X-rayed. Nothing showed up on the X-ray except that there was an abnormality in his lungs—he vet had caught a glimpse of the bottom of Freckle's lungs while taking pictures of his back bone. We thought he had pneumonia and maybe had strained his back. The second possibility was cancer that had metastasized to his lungs.

I opted for the first diagnosis but the reality was that he did have cancer. It was a quick realization. He got worse and worse in just a few days and, of course, he was miserable.

We sadly and finally decided it as his time to leave us. That day, we gave him a huge breakfast: sausage, eggs, pancakes, syrup, lots of butter and milk. We then took him to the vet happy and full, and wished him a safe journey from his short life of pain and misery.

He was such a nice, mild tempered boy.

I miss him every day.

HAMILTON

Hamilton was in the dog pound. Someone had kicked him like a football across the room and he could not walk when we went to rescue him from the animal control.

He was just a puppy and it is beyond me how someone could kick one across the room. I suspect it was probably because he messed in the house, but a compassionate person does not treat any living soul like that, especially a young dog. And then, to take him to the local animal control because you thought you broke his leg instead of taking him to the veterinarian—that's just tossing him aside like an old dirty dish rag; making the decision to put this young puppy to sleep instead of trying to repair the damage that you did to him. This type of thinking is just beyond my comprehension.

One of our foster homes volunteered to take care of Hamilton. As soon as she got him she rushed him to her local vet. Hamilton's foster mom thought he had a broken hip, and her vet confirmed it.

Hamilton had problems with his bladder, too. He could not hold his urine. Perhaps that was from a bruised kidney; we were not sure.

Our rescue vet is an orthopedic surgeon and he gives rescue a 25% discount, so we got Hamilton's X-Rays from the foster mom's vet, and took Hamilton to our vet to fix his hip.

Our rescue vet he said the boy did not have a broken hip; it was just a sprained knee and hip. He had looked at the same X rays the other vet had taken, and said. "These do not show a break." So we treated Hamilton with pain killers, and tried to keep him calm and resting so the hip could heal.

Hamilton was taken outside to potty on a leash so he would not bolt off after squirrels or rabbits and hurt his leg more.

Weeks went by and Hamilton began to heal. He hobbled along for a long time before his hip and knee healed. But, when they did, he was like a bolt of lightning making up for all of the mischief he had missed the weeks he was restrained. Although, he will always have a slight problem holding his urine.

A wonderful older man read about Hamilton on the Daily Drool and fell in love with him. He adopted Hamilton to keep him company on his long work trips driving between Louisiana and

Kansas City.

But after a few tries taking Hamilton on the trips, he was forced to leave him home with his wife. Hamilton could not hold his urine as long as was needed during traveling.

After a few years, Hamilton's bladder healed and he was able to travel again.

Hamilton now enjoys a pain free life with his loving master.

HAPPY

The only part of Happy that looks like a Basset is his tail! He is closer to a blue tick coon hound than a Basset.

For days, I'd see him in the street while driving back and forth to work. I'd stop, put him back in his yard, close the gate, and wish him well. And each day as I drove by, there he was again in the street. So, one day I took him to the door of his home and said to his owners:

"You keep opening the gate to your fence and your dog is wandering in the street every morning and every evening when I drive by on my way to work." The lady looked puzzled as if to say

"Why didn't you just put him back in my yard and close the gate like you have every day for the past two weeks instead of bothering me with this?"

After a pause the lady said, "It is the kid's dog. If they forget to shut the gate and he wanders, I could care less," she explained. "It is up to them to make sure he is safe." It seemed she took no responsibility at all for her dog.

I told her that, in fact, she is responsible for him. She is the mother of children who need to be taught responsibility and that evidently she was not doing a very good job of it. With that, she took Happy into the house and I left.

The next day I did not see him in the morning as I drove by, although I did see her gate wide open again. That evening, Happy was once again there in the street. So, I picked him up and brought him home with me. The next day I went by the house and told the lady I took the dog home. "If you want him back, give me a call. "

She never did.

We named him Happy because he always seems to be smiling. He is always nice—doesn't have a mean bone in his whole body. He is cordial to every dog we invite him to play with, and he is never ever aggressive. He is always just what his name states: Happy. He does not care where he is or what you expect of him. He will never disappoint anyone. He is just Happy to be loved and cared for.

Happy has been in rescue since 2005. We think he was six when we picked him up. He has never been able to be adopted into a forever home for long because, unfortunately, he marks inside the home. So, we placed him in a foster home, hoping he would eventually be adopted. However, he has been in the same foster home now for so many years that it is home to him. He used to live with two other Bassets and a terrier. The two other Bassets have since passed away and now Brandy, his canine sister, is his companion—both waiting for "Mom" to get home from school to get lots of love and attention. Since their mom is a teacher, she has all summer to spoil Happy and Brandy—and she does just that.

Happy has had his share of medical problems. He was not neutered when we took him in, so he needed to be fixed. His teeth were rotting, so they needed to be cleaned. He had some cysts and they needed to be removed. Ear infections, which are pretty normal for a dog that spent most of his life ignored and allowed to walk the streets, were also a problem.

But most recently he was diagnosed with Cushing's. Cushing's is a cancer of the adrenal gland, causing it to malfunction. Cushing's can be debilitating and can even cause death. However, with proper medication Happy will live a few more years. He enjoys being outside, but lounges inside during the day while his mom is at school teaching. When she comes home, he goes outside to play and then comes back in for a petting session and dinner. He is always Happy for any attention he can get.

The past few months Happy is having trouble walking and now needs help to get around. We have to use a beach towel to hold him up and help him walk. But he does not mind. He is just as Happy as ever, with no fears and no worries—this is just a good life for him.

Happy is a very peaceable loving dog that has had a second chance at being cared for in the loving arms of a rescue volunteer.

JO JO

The day we got Jo Jo was a sunny warm day. We were told there was going to be an auction- few puppy millers were selling their stock and there were going to be sixteen Bassets up for bid.

"Do not let them know you are with a rescue though or they will hike the bid on you," we were advised. So, we drove almost 200 miles to rescue those sixteen Bassets from the horrible life of living in a puppy mill.

It was so sickening to watch these ruthless people putting all of these frightened dogs up on a table to be glared upon by a room full of bidders.

There was one Chihuahua who was in labor while she was on the stand being bid on. I found out later that she and the pups were fine. Fine, except in about six weeks the pups would be off to some pet store someplace for sale and the mother caged until she came into heat again. It was so sad.

Jo Jo Bear came up first; she was the first Basset up on the block. We spent $450.00 for her. We were sunk—they knew we were not millers; millers do not bid that high. We were suppose to let the first dog go and not bid it up, since the first dog is always the test to see how high you will bid. The millers judge you by how much you will spend. We learned that lesson that hard way, but they wanted our money and we wanted as many Bassets as we could save with the money we had left. We kept bidding until the money was gone. We ended up getting only five Bassets for the $1600.00 we brought with us. The other eleven were still left in the system.

We had had nothing to eat or drink all day. So, as we headed home we decided to stop at a fast-food restaurant to get drinks. As my husband opened the truck door, Jo Jo shot out the door...

"Oh no! Now what!?!" We chased her and chased her around a field in Southern Missouri for four and a half hours. We had people from the highway and people from the nearby restaurant all trying to help us round her up, but she kept slipping by us all until she finally got tired and just gave up

It was dark before we got home and finally got the dogs settled and enjoyed a meal. We notified the foster homes that we had lined up to take the dogs--they would be delivered the next day. We had a foster home lined up for Jo Jo, but Jo Jo had become endeared to my husband as she tried to give him a heart attack by chasing her for hours. He decided we would foster her. After all the trouble we went through to keep her safe, he deserved the right to keep Jo Jo at our house. She was going to stay with him. And, after ten years, she is still here in our home.

Jo Jo still pretends to be frightened. It has become a game with her. She barely lets us pet the tip of her nose and wiggles away like one of those vibrating toys you set on the floor and it shimmies across the room as it vibrates. However, when we leave the gate open, she will not leave. She is more afraid of what is beyond the gate than of where she lives.

She is grateful to be in Rescue, because Rescue is safe.

LOONEY

A voice on the other end of the phone says, "We have a Basset Hound we can no longer keep. We took it from a neighbor who lost their home. We were going to keep her for them, but they decided they no longer want her and she poops too big for me to keep the yard clean, I am sick."

I get the address, loaded up my car and away I went to Kansas City, Kansas. The house looked like a mansion, with statues outside and a courtyard--a very pretty home. I rang the bell and the woman came to the door. A frail man hobbled down the hall, as I entered their home. Down the hall, two dogs—a small, yappy one and a Basset Hound who is snarling and showing her teeth.

"That is Luna," the man says. "I really love her." I hear this same phrase every time I go on a rescue. "But I am very ill and it takes too much out of me to clean her poop out of the yard."

Okay. Never heard that line before. I must add it to my growing list of dumb excuses. I get both the man and the woman to sign the owner release form. They put the harness I brought on Luna for me since she is still snapping at me. All the while I am asking myself, "What I am going to do with a dog like this?"

I drag her reluctant little body towards my car and reach down to put her in the back seat and...Snap! Snap! Snap! I wish I had brought a muzzle, as well.

The man says, "Here, let me help you." And he gives her a boost into the car.

Okay, so there I was in the car. This dog that bites was in the car, too. And I have to drive home with her. Fortunately, the ride went well. And, fortunately, when I got there, my husband had just gotten home from work. So, he helps me get her out of the car. We take her into our bedroom. Along the way, she is snapping at all of the dogs and at us as we escort her through the house.

That is when my husband changed her name from Luna to Looney. It just seemed to fit not only her demeanor, but our state of mind.

Looney jumped on our bed and settled down and all was

well until bedtime. She bit us both as we tried to crawl into bed— my husband worse than me. However, he did manage to grab her around her waist and drew her back close to him He hugged her and whispered softly, "It's okay. You are going to be fine." He held her even though blood was running down his arm, and rubbed her belly. Finally, she started to calm down. She slept with us—or, should I say, she let us sleep with her. The rest of the night went well. No more bloodshed.

The bed became her personal lair. Whenever we would go near it, she would show her teeth and growl at us. She also protected it from other Basset invasions. As long as we left her alone all was good.

One day I needed to trim her toenails, so I got out the muzzle just to be safe, after all we had been through a similar experience with Rocky our second rescue. When she saw the muzzle, she rolled over on the bed stuck her feet straight up in the air, and snarled at me. But she did let me clip her toenails, albeit with some snapping, but they were just warning snaps. No blood was drawn. Wow! I was impressed. I showed Jim what had happened.

"Look!" I exclaimed, got out the toenail clippers, and showed them to Looney. She dropped onto the bed and slowly rolled over onto her back, snarling and showing her teeth the whole time. She stuck her toe bones straight up into the air. We both had to laugh—it was the funniest thing you ever saw.

Looney still sleeps with us. She stays in the bed almost all day long. It is her safe haven. Yet, she will come out every now and then to mingle with the other dogs. Oh, and at meal time she wants to sit right next to me and beg. I admit I am a softy, so she does get a few table scraps. She now lets me clean her ears and clip her nails, although there is much snarling involved. She also initiates petting now. It is evident that she loves us as much as we love her.

I became so comfortable with her growling after five years, that when, a few weeks ago, she was eating a dog biscuit on the bed .I wanted to play, so I decided to take it from her to be cute. My husband said, "Don't tease her or you will be sorry!" But I reached anyway, saying, "She will not bite me."

Ooops. Wrong move. She bit me on the bottom knuckle of my right-hand index finger, puncturing both sides. The bite was deep to the bone. I decided that that was a dumb move on my part, teasing her like that.

Even though she has been with us for so long, she still has her moments.

However, she but she is daddy's little girl, his princess. The guarder of the bed. I have had a few applications on her, but we need to find her an adopter who really knows and understands a crazy dog like her: someone without kids, someone tolerant, someone just like us.

She probably will never find another home, but she is okay with us. We all fit right in together. Some dogs will never leave rescue, but to them this is home.

LUKE

Luke's story also comes from our fellow canine rescuer, Marie Campbell.

I hope this story doesn't bore you, but I feel compelled to tell you my boy Luke's story. I adopted Luke in May of 2011 from the Human Society of Tampa Bay. This is a weird story, so I hope you will bear with me.

I have always been a dog person—I was born into a dog family. My grandparents always had 12 dogs or more, including purebreds and rescues. My dad is a one-dog man, but very loyal. I have always had a mix of purchased purebreds and rescues.

I have been in rescue and have bred and shown dogs for over 17 years. Guess I am a dog nut.

WEEEELLLL...in May of 20011, I had this weird dream. It was about a lemon and white Basset boy in a shelter that I needed to go adopt. I saw him in chain link run, his coloring clearly, the PVC bed he was lying on, and I even knew he was male, and that I was supposed to go adopt him. Now, until this time, I had never even seen a lemon and white Basset. So, this was doubly strange. I told my mother all about my dream in the morning and laughed because the last thing I needed was another dog!!! I also never have this kind of vivid dream, so I didn't take it seriously. I just shook it off and ignored it

A week later, the humane society announced that they were taking in 200 dogs from the Mississippi floods. They were urging everyone to come and adopt, panning the camera through the shelter. Low and behold, guess who my mom saw??? Luke in a run laying on a PVC bed. She called me in to see him on the TV. We just looked at each other and said, "I guess we better go get him!!!"

We showed up on Monday to adopt him, hoping he was still there. The day they made the announcement, 150 dogs were adopted and we didn't see Luke until the 11:00 PM news Saturday night. Sure enough, we get there and Luke was still available. They were calling him Fusby. Why? I have no idea. Anyway, I filled out the application, passed all the background checks, and got approved for adoption. The kennel manager sent an attendant back to go get the Basset...but he was gone.

Apparently, a lady from the shelter board of directors took him from the facility for public education—supposedly to tour schools to show kids how to take care of pets. The manager informed me that he was still mine and would be back at the facility for me to pick up in 24 hours.

Well, 24 hours came and went, and Luke still had not been returned. The manager called me, apologized, and said he would be returned in 24 hours. Thursday rolled around and the manager had to call the director and demand Luke's return--he was somebody else's dog and that the shelter no longer owned him.

The lady finally returned him and I showed up to pick Luke up. While waiting for them to finish his paper work and to service other people, I sneaked in the back and finally got to see him in person. Luke was lying on his PVC bed staring straight ahead and wouldn't make eye contact.

He had been shaved from his neck to his privates and all four legs were also shaved. On his sides, he was covered with medical cuts and scrapes where, I learned, they had practiced testing him for allergies. All four of his legs were punctured where practice IV lines had been run. He was also painfully thin—25 pounds under weight--and his hips and ribs were sticking out four inches on all sides with his skin stretched over them. He had to lay on padded dog beds and blankets because he was so thin.

The director hadn't taken him out for public education. She was taking him to the University of Florida College of Veterinary Medicine so that interns could practice procedures on him. This painfully thin, sad angel had been subjected to further torture and misery after his ordeal of being nearly starved to death by his owners, who mercifully abandon him during the floods and then was transported from Mississippi to Florida. The floods had nothing to do with him being 25 pounds under weight. His owners just decided to stop feeding him, and when they were evacuated from their home, they abandoned him to fend for himself. He was found wandering the street.

The shelter manager took me aside for a "talk" to explain his condition before bringing him out. They did not know that I had already sneaked a peek at him. When they brought him to me, he went nuts with excitement. He was so thin and shaved and pitiful. He broke my heart.

We also learned that he had been a breeder's dog and kept in a cement run. He did not even know what grass was. He was used to walk in six- foot patterns before he realized he could run around in my whole fenced-in acre. He used to just sit and watch people walk by and wag his tail. He never barked. But he is now a wonderful talker!!!

The first week I owned Luke, he stole a large bag of dinner rolls from off the stove and I ran after him trying to catch him. When I got to him, he dropped the rolls and started to scream. I then knew someone used to chase him down and beat him. It makes me cry just to remember it.

Now, he is so perfect. He sleeps with me and my other Basset, Fancy, on my bed every night. He is my sweet-hearted angel and my Mississippi Man. The funny thing is, he came to and acknowledged his name, Luke, immediately. My Dad and stepmom couldn't believe it. He is now at his ideal weight of 65 pounds and, as I said, perfect.

Anyway, that is our story.

I think the dream was about him needing to be rescued from the testing at the University of Florida. The university keeps dogs for testing, and I have no doubt in my mind that the director would have left him there. I know this sounds nuts, but it is what I believe.

I hope this story didn't creep you out or bore you. All three of my bassets are rescue with odd stories but I am so grateful to have them. They rule my Newfoundlands with an iron fist! HAHAHAHA!

MILLIE

     To finance our rescue, I used to work in a nursing home. My husband and I would spend nearly $20,000 a year on veterinarian bills for the rescue dogs out of our own pocket. We have hardly anything to show for the money we spent—except healthy, happy dogs.

     One day at work, a housekeeper came up to me and said, "You rescue Bassets, don't you?"

     "Yes I do," I said.

     She proceeded to tell me a story about how her daughter was in a store and next door to the store in there was an older

Basset trying to go into a tattoo shop; she thought maybe it wanted to get out of the heat; it was one of those 105-degree Missouri Summer days. Then she saw this man kick the dog out of the shop.

So, she took the Basset home, She and her family were going to try to keep her, but one of the children was allergic. The housekeeper asked if I would take the dog. And, of course, I said yes.

I got the daughters phone number and address and went to see the dog. She wagged her tail and looked so hopeful when I came to get her. As soon as I saw her, I knew her name was going to be Millie. She just spoke to me with her eyes—she loved the name Millie.

I am not sure the bumps on the child were from being allergic to the dog, because the Basset was loaded with fleas. The fleas were so bad that she almost looked grayish in color. She was also emaciated and looked very sickly. I did not tell the woman I thought her son had flea bites all over him because I might have been wrong. But they did have a cat and one or two other dogs. However, I did tell her that Millie was loaded with fleas and she needed to get her other animals treated before the fleas totally infested her home.

I scooped Millie up and took her straight to my veterinarian. The first thing he did was treat her for fleas. During treatment, the pests dropped off of her and the pile looked like a big mud pie sitting there on the floor like an outline of her body.

Next, because she winced in pain, I had Millie examined

and an X-ray. I told the vet she had been kicked by the owner of a tattoo parlor. Luckily, she had no broken bones but her spleen was torn. Within the next few days, Millie had her spleen removed.

Millie was with us six years before she developed cancer and she had to have another operation to have the cancer taken care of. The results were good—she was cancer free.

Millie was finally adopted by an older man whose dear Basset girl was lost to The Bridge. Millie is now living with the gentleman and his older daughter.

Her "new" owner has since retired and now devotes all of his time to giving Millie the best years of her life.

MILTON

The story of Milton is a rescue failure.

Milton seemed like such a nice boy. He was found as a stray and brought to rescue. Milton stayed mostly to himself. We thought he was shy, but who knows what demons were lurking inside his mind? What has his past been like? Sometimes you wish you knew just what an animal was thinking—or do they think at all?

Milton was in rescue only a few weeks when he was adopted by a nice young family. They took good care of Milton and he seemed to blossom.

The couple had two young girls who loved to play with Milton and he fit right into his new home.

One day we got a call. We needed to come pick Milton up as soon as possible.

I drove out to the country where Milton lived. It was winter and so very dark, I almost missed the street they lived on, but thank goodness for cell phones. I got turned around and finally got to Milton's new home to take him back into rescue.

Milton had snapped at one of the girls.

Wow! I never saw that coming. He seemed like such a well-balanced boy.

Well, I thought to myself, maybe the girl pulled his tail or ears. Maybe it was just a warning and the dad was overprotective of his girls. Who knew? But I put Milton in my car and we headed back home to my house, thing that I would find him another home. Maybe one with older children who know how to interact with a dog.

A few days later, it was treat time and Milton, who usually stayed curled up on the couch where I had to take his treats to him, was in the crowd of hungry Bassets waiting their turn for a cookie.

Milton turned and snapped at another Basset that got too close. I said, "No, Milton!"

Milton's eyes changed from a soft Brown to a glowing orange. His lips curled up and he started to snarl at me. I just turned my back and walked away from him, thinking he was having a bad day.

A few days later this same scenario happened, but this time when I said, "No Milton!" he changed. He charged at me, lunging forward and grabbing my jeans. He took about a teaspoon of flesh out of my upper thigh, tearing through the jeans with his razor-like teeth.

A few moments later he was snuggled up on the couch like nothing had ever happened.

You think I would have learned my lesson, but I thought it was just a fluke; it will not happen again. A few more days pass and I dropped a piece of meat on the floor as I was fixing my lunch. Milton and another dog started growling at each other. So, without thinking, "No!" comes blurting from my mouth again. Milton's demeanor changed in an instant. Hs eyes glowed, his teeth showing. He lunged and tore my jeans again and took a tablespoon size piece of hide from my upper thigh. Then he did it again—lunged for me. But, this time, but I jumped back and he missed. He was backing me into a corner. I put my hands out to stop him as he lunged the third time.

This was the worst idea I ever came up with.

He attacked my fingers and I came back with three dangling finger tips. I turned and got a trash can sitting next to me to place between him and I. I ran for the bathroom where I taped up my fingertips--gluing them back in place with some steri-strips I had in my drawer. I then changed my clothes and left for work. As I walked by the couch, there he was—all cute and snuggled in, wagging his tail as I went out the door.

I worked at a nursing home and there the nurses helped me clean my wounds and put more steri-strips on that I brought to work with me. That should do for a day or two, but what to do with Milton? I took Milton to the veterinarian and told them what was happening. They tested him and discovered he had a brain disease known as idiopathic aggression, commonly known as rage syndrome. Milton could not help what he was doing, but he was a danger to everyone around him.

We had to make a hard decision. We had to send Milton and his demons on their way. He was so peaceful as he slipped away. He looked at me and thanked me for helping him. I felt so sad for him, but it was a dangerous disease and not one that could be cured.

This was my rescue failure. I am so sorry, Milton. I wish I could have taken your demons away so that you could still be with us.

MOLLY AND STINKY PEET

Molly

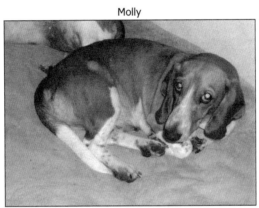

Stinky Peet

Stinky Peet is a young Basset who was born into rescue, one of four puppies. We rescued her mom, Molly, from death row at the Kansas City Animal Control before she had her litter.

When we picked up Molly, she tried to bite everyone in sight, so we had to muzzle her to get her from her cage at animal control into our car before I released the muzzle. This was a very bad idea. I decided I was not too smart for releasing the muzzle when I found after driving her two miles to my home that she chewed the back seatbelts in half. From then on I had to tie knots in my seatbelts to be able to put them on. It was a good thing I only used that car to haul dogs in. No one else would ride in it with me.

A week later, the four puppies were born—Molly being pregnant was the reason she was so afraid and protective. The puppies were not purebred Basset puppies, but they were cute and they were Molly's, and after they were born, she was very protective of them.

The foster home named Stinky's momma Widget, so the puppies when they came here were named Widget One, Widget Two, Three, and Four. I thought that was pretty cute and left them that way as long as they were in foster care. The foster mom found good homes for the babies, and three of the four puppies were adopted. That left one puppy and the momma dog.

Stinky Peet's siblings, one male and two females, got great homes. The male was adopted by vet tech and one female was adopted by another vet tech from the clinic the foster home used. And a young family got the other female. That left the foster with

Widget and one pup.

My husband and I needed to take the remaining two dogs to our house because once her puppies left, the momma dog started running away from the foster home looking for the other pups. When the two came to our house to stay, my husband renamed Widget to Molly (as the Mommy of the babies. Molly/Mommy; they rhymed). We renamed the Widget pup Stinky Peet.

Stinky Pet and Molly, her mom, are still here in rescue.

Stinky Peet was the rascal of the bunch. She took on her mom's personality—very frightened of people, but standing up for herself. While all of the other puppies found great homes, Stinky Peet was so scared of any change in her routine that she was not adoptable. Every time anything is moved or changed, she gets very nervous and hides. For example, one night it was cooler outside, so we moved a fan over by the window to bring the cool night air into our bedroom as we slept. She shivered and shrieked until we moved the fan back where it was suppose to be. Then she settled in. If we take her to the vet, she shivers and almost goes catatonic from fear of being out of her normal environment.

I first started calling her Stinker because Jim would roll her over on his lap and rub her feet to tease me because she will not let me trim her toenails without a real fight. I started telling her, "I am gonna get those Peet (feet)" and pretty soon I just started calling her Stinky Peet and it stuck.

She was a pretty good puppy as puppies go, not getting into much. She loved chewing on her dog bones, and she was not a lot of trouble as most puppies can be. But all of a sudden she started chewing on cloth. She would chew on the couch just a little around the bottom fringe and she would chew on the couch covers.

One morning, my husband woke up and heard a faint whimper and a soft woof. He looked and looked and could not find where it was coming from. He then noticed one of the dog beds was moving. There was a dog bed moving by itself and the very soft woof coming from the vicinity of the bed. He kept looking at it and saw a snout peeking out of a small hole in the corner of the bed. Stinky Peet had chewed a hole in the dog bed, had chewed her way into the bed, and was now stuck. She had been chewing on that bed for days and I kept vowing to sew it with metal thread to fix it so that she could not spread stuffing-like snow all over the house, but I kept procrastinating and never got that done.

Now she has chewed her way into the bed. My husband unzipped the zipper and dug her out. She never touched the bed again. We were very fortunate that she did not suffocate. It was scary on both our parts—hers and ours—but, like I said, she never chewed on a dog bed again. Now it is sheets she loves to tear; the sheets on our bed! It drives me crazy. But at least she cannot get trapped and is safe. That is more important to us than anything.

Stinky Peet is over a year now and weighs only 24 pounds. She is tiny compared to most Bassets and she sleeps between her daddy and me on the bed. She is one of the three Bassets that share our bed at night, with me hanging over the edge on one side and my husband spending half the night in our whirlpool bathtub because the Bassets are turned sideways, stretched out from nose to tail as far as they can reach. Stinky Peet is the only one curled into a ball, snuggled up close. She is a delight to have among all of the older Bassets in our home, always entertaining us.

We would love to be able to find her a good home, but, for now, she has this home she calls her own.

She is a doll.

PICKLES

This Basset Puppy was found dragging along beside the edge of a small lake. It was likely that someone tried to drown her. A passerby picked her up and took her to the Lawrence Kansas Humane Society.

Pickles was only about five or six weeks old, practically frozen, close to death. The Humane Society had to put her on IVs in the hospital for a month, and then they called us and asked if we had room for a two-and-a-half month-old puppy.

When we got her, she was so small--only about seven

pounds. She was very tiny, not even as long as my forearm. When she came to us, she was still on antibiotics, diagnosed with severe pneumonia. Her lungs were full of fluid; that is why we think someone had tried to drown her.

We could not get her spayed until she was almost four months old because she was just not strong enough.

Pickles slept with us and became very protective of her "mommy" and "daddy", even though she was just a little fart, she would growl and act like a wolverine when another dog would pass by. She curled up in a tight ball in the middle f the bed each night with us and would not move a muscle.

When we first got Pickles we had linoleum on our bathroom and kitchen floors. Pickles did not like linoleum. She would find a small spot and work on the linoleum until she created a very tiny hole. Three days later, the linoleum was shredded like cheese. Soon I just had wood flooring in the kitchen and bathroom.

She loved to play a game with Daisey Mae, an eleven-year-old female. Every time Pickles tried to cross Daisy's path, Pickles would whine and squeal and act like Daisey was killing her. Then she would roll onto her back and puff up her belly in the air and be submissive. Daisey loved that game. As a little old lady she did not get the upper hand on very many of the dogs, but Pickles knew she deserved respect and she gave it to her by letting Daisey feel like she was still the leader of the pack.

Pickles was a good hunter. She would go out into the yard, sit behind a tree, and watch and wait for hours. She caught a bird once and proudly brought it to me. Once she caught a baby rabbit, but we made her let it go. She was always a very busy girl.

After Pickles was well and spayed, I really wanted to keep her. We had been through so much with her. But I knew if I kept this sweet girl, she would be taking the room I would have to save one more. As a rescue, our main goal is to re-home these precious dogs. So, we advertised her on Petfinder.com and soon Pickles was in her new home.

I remember how confused she looked at me as I left her behind with a new family, but she is doing well, now. I felt bad about leaving her, but it was for the best. She would be able to get much more attention in her new home and I would have room to help another needy Basset.

ROSCOE

Roscoe's master was put in a nursing home and the daughter of the man did not want his dogs. She was going to take them to the Animal Control, but a friend of hers talked her into bringing them to Rescue. He had two Bassets, Roscoe and Boscoe. Both dogs were 10 years old.

The dogs had been well cared for most of their lives, but as their owner's mental decline started a few years ago, their vetting needs were put on the back burner. The owner could not remember that they needed shots; need their ears and teeth cleaned, toenails trimmed, as well as baths. He did remember to feed them daily, which was a good thing. They were fairly healthy when we got them.

Roscoe's teeth were not in good shape. He had to have several pulled just after we got him. The daughter of the man who gave them to us said she would gladly pay us back any vetting the dogs needed, but she never did. She owned a huge trucking company in Iowa and she promised to donate to us for taking the dogs since her father had loved them so and she was so grateful we took them in; but she never did that, either.

Weekly, I sent her pictures of the boys and how good they were doing that she took to her father. She would email me that it was the only thing that made him smile and thanked me for making his days brighter. However, he never knew the dogs were in rescue. He thought the daughter still had his dogs at her home and she was caring for them. She felt he would be upset to know she gave them away, since he was so attached to the boys.

Boscoe died a few months after we got him; he seemed to be the older more frail one of the two, although I was told Roscoe was the oldest.

Roscoe was a beautiful almost pure white—a very rare color—Basset. And he was so gentle and sweet. I knew we would probably keep him till he passed on, but then we got an email from Ozark Mountain Basset Rescue. They had a previous adopter who was interested in Roscoe. She applied to give him a home in Arkansas. Since one of the directors of Ozark Mountain Basset Rescue highly recommended this adopter, we loaded Roscoe into the car and drove part way to Arkansas to meet her and let her see him.

It was love at first sight. Roscoe took to the woman like she was a long, lost friend he was meeting with after years of separation. The woman adored him, swooped him up into her arms, caressed him, and then put him in her car where she had on top of the front seat for him to lay in a soft bed filled with treats and toys to keep him company on her long way home.

She emailed me several days in a row after Roscoe went to live with her, thanking us for letting her adopt him and that he had become the center of her world. He loved the yard they had. He would lay out there in the cool Autumn breezes, watching birds and possum play. When he was tired, he would mosey through the dog door and come inside to lay on one of the many dog beds in each room of her house. He made himself right at home with her like he had lived there forever and, to this day, is still enjoying his new forever home.

I emailed his former owner that Roscoe got a good home. She was glad to know. Her father was failing and did not even remember that he had dogs or children by now. It is sad when people lose themselves and dogs lose their homes. But all turned out well for Roscoe—a great dog with a second chance in a wonderful home.

ROSIE/PEPPER

Friday evening at 8:00 we were called by a couple in Overland Park. There was a young Basset Hound running down 95th and Antioch. The couple picked her up and took her to their home, but could not keep her. They asked us to come pick her up from Overland Park. We went to get her and discovered that she had either just had pups or had had a false pregnancy—she had milk and her belly sagged. I was so afraid she had left pups somewhere, but there was nothing we could do but take her to our home and wait, hoping that, if she had pups, they were weaned.

I posted to every lost dog registry in the area and to all the pounds that we had found a lost Basset Hound. I even posted on Craig's list! I called the Overland Park Animal Control first thing Monday and told them if anyone called, we had a lost Basset taken from the 95th and Antioch neighborhood. This dog was very sweet and slept with my husband. She was so beautiful and had such a sweet face that I named her Rosie.

I found out later that her name was actually Pepper.

We had Rosie/Pepper five days. She was finally getting comfortable with us and was initiating play from our other hounds. She was a jewel and I really became attached to her sweet personality in that short time.

A man called us on Tuesday and told us where he thought the dog lived, so I asked him to put a note on the door for the owners to call us.

I took the dog to the vet to see if she was micro-chipped, got her shots and had her heartworm tested. Then, Wednesday, at noon, the man who owned the dog called me and left a message. I was at the hospital with a friend when he called and did not get home till five that evening. When I listened to his voice mail, the background noise sounded like he was in a bar, but it could have just been a loud restaurant. In any event, I promptly returned his call.

This man started yelling at me as soon as he answered the phone. He said he was not coming clear over to Raytown for "the stupid dog" and told me to "keep the darn thing". This is a watered-down version—his speech was full of cussing and much worse words. I asked him if I could meet him somewhere—he could drive part way…He only cussed some more. I mentioned to him that we were a rescue and we got her shots. Then I politely asked him if he would reimburse us. He said many more bad words and then threatened me and my husband's life.

"You can keep the dog," he said and then hung up.

Next, we get a call from the wife, who yelled and screamed, saying that her children missed the dog and that we were thieves. My husband asked her to calm down.

"Please, just listen to us," Jim said.

She said, "I want my dog back. You're trying to steal it and demanding money from me." She was almost as belligerent as her husband. I was afraid for my own husband, myself, and the dog, but we tried to work things out the best we could.

We asked for proof. They emailed us a picture and it was their dog.

Since the husband threatened my husband and myself, we were was afraid to meet them. So, we called the police and told them the situation. They told us to call the people back and meet them at the police station with the dog. We would have an officer there to protect us.

When we met them, the people acted like spoiled children. I did not want to give them Rosie/Pepper. I did not think they deserved the dog back, but we had to. The husband was giving us "the finger" and cussing at us while the wife was telling the police officer their side of the story—which was all lies. She called us a few names, too, but she had two children in the back seat of their car, and the sweet dog was happy to see the kids.

I just hope they take care of the dog. I did not sleep that night because of this. I want the best for every dog, and I hated to see this sweet dog returned to those ugly people.

This is the heartbreak of rescue.

Now this woman has posted on Facebook that we are a scam stealing dogs and is asking for money. She put some twisted lies on there invented by her own imagination. I just told her I was sorry we had a miscommunication and that I hoped her dog brought joy to their home again.

SAMMY

It was a cold October Friday in 2005 when we got Sammy. The phone rang and my husband answered. It was the Independence Animal Control. They had a Basset that had been hit by a car, and it sounded like it had kennel cough. My husband rushed to the Animal Control. When he got there, one of the officers told him that a lady driving to work saw a car hit the dog. He was thrown up into the air across the street and fell into a storm drain. She saw the whole thing and stopped, but could not get the dog out of the drain. He was stuck and was not moving his back legs—she thought they were broken.

We got him out of the drain and brought him here, but he kept on coughing, an indication of kennel cough. My husband said, "I will take him to my vet and get him checked out." And so, we took Sammy into our rescue.

Our vet was out of town, so Jim had to settle on taking him to an alternate vet, who said he thought the dog had a cold. He sent him home with my husband, along with some antibiotics.

The next day was Saturday. We were worried about the dog's breathing and were sure he was in need of some medical help. So we took him to another vet that very afternoon.

This vet looked into Sammy's records and said, "I think he has something wrong with his lungs."

I told her that after he eats he can hardly breathe—he obviously was eating much. I was worried; he looked to only be about six months old. She said the vet that saw him the day before put "possible Distemper" in his records. I was furious. "Possible distemper? He thought this dog had distemper, but did not tell us and let a dog with distemper to taken into my home to mingle with twelve other dogs who were healthy?" I was so mad I could hardly see straight. I never went back to that vet again, but that is another story.

The vet I was seeing now said, "I do not think he has distemper, so don't worry. But he does have something wrong with his lungs--maybe a hernia. Wait till Monday and come in and see Dr. Chirpich. He is an expert with hernias."

We took Sammy back home and his conditioned worsened.

By Monday morning, he could hardly breathe. By that time, I had decided to stop his suffering and put him to sleep. I called Dr Chirpich, who was back in his office and said, "I am bringing in a dog to be put to sleep."

When we saw Dr. Chirpich and told him Sammy's story, he said, "He has a hernia. His guts were pushed into his lung cavity from being hit by the car and he needs surgery immediately. However, he is going to be fine." Six hours later Sammy was breathing fine. His legs had been bruised and out of their sockets, and the doc fixed them, too. After sixty some stitches and three hours of surgery, Sammy was going to be okay.

Sammy was placed in a foster home with no other dogs to get well--he was supposed to be quiet for three weeks while he healed. After that, he came back to our house and became spoiled rotten. He was always special to us because of his rough start in rescue, but he finally found a wonderful home with a family with three boys. Sammy fell in love with them and they with him.

Rescue is rewarding.

SARAH

Sarah was a young female puppy, about four months old. We had four puppies from the same litter but only Sarah showed signs of not feeling well. As the day wore on, she could not keep any food or fluids down. We were battling diarrhea and vomiting time after time I knew this was dangerous for Sarah because puppies are so vulnerable to getting dehydrated.

I called my emergency veterinarian's number and he met us at the clinic on Sunday. We decided Sarah needed IVs and antibiotics. Since I had experience giving meds to people, the vet gave me everything that I needed to put Sarah on IVs at home. However, he did warn me to keep her separated from the rest of the dogs and to bleach everything she came in contact with.

"Bring her back to the clinic on Monday," he said.

We were giving Sarah IV antibiotics and fluids round the clock, but she seemed just to get worse and worse.

Monday came and we took her to the vet clinic. She was so weak; she could not even hold her head up.

The vet said, "I am afraid Sarah has Parvo."

Parvo to puppies is like a death sentence, very few survive. And all of the other dogs and three puppies at my house were all exposed—so more may be getting sick later.

They took Sarah and put her in a sanitary room at the vet's office and started stronger IV medications. I asked the vet if I could stay with her by her side and he said, "Sure, but make sure if you touch her to wash your hands with bleach, and take your clothes off and wash them as soon as you get home so that you do not expose the other dogs to more viruses."

I stayed with Sarah as long as I could, then went home to a night of tossing and turning—worrying whether or not she would still be alive in the morning and whether or not any of the 21 other dogs I currently had were going to develop the virus.

Next morning, I had to go to work but rushed right back to Sarah's side as soon as I could. She was not doing well; the virus had gone to her lungs. Her little nose was all snotty and breathing was labored. She was thin and very frail. I worried again all that night long.

Should I keep trying or let her go?

The next day, I went to the vet's early before I went to work. I could see a spark in her eyes and even though she seemed to be slipping away, for the first time I had some glimmer of hope that she might make it.

While I was at work, he vet called my husband around 1:00 that afternoon and said he thought it would be best to put Sarah to sleep. Jim husband called me at work and told me what the vet said. I said I want to see her one more time.

"Let me go see her after work and I will decide." Everyone agreed.

When I got to the vet's after work, I sat there praying what to do. And then, Sarah wagged her tail. She had been too weak to wag her tail before, but now she started to wag it! I cleaned the snot off her nose, put some Vaseline on her poor raw snout, kissed her, held her petted her, and decided she was still fighting to stay alive. The vet disagreed with me but, upheld my wishes.

The next morning, Sarah was standing and starting to eat. She had a long way to go. She was weak, but she was still very determined to stay here with me.

Every spare moment I had, I kept visiting her every day, and she got better and better each day. My vet did not believe his eyes. He said he was so happy that she was getting better. He was so glad that I made the decision not to put her down, even when he thought it was the only thing to do. He exclaimed he was "so happy to be wrong!"

Sarah made it through the bout of Parvo and, miraculously, no one else got sick. Sarah got a great permanent home with a little girl and her family. They sent me a picture of the little girl and Sarah standing at a window looking out at the snow falling, the little girl with her arm around Sarah. What a wonderful life she has now. She fought hard to get well and lived happily ever after.

Sarah will always have a special place in my heart. Because of her, I will be determined to keep fighting to keep all of the dogs in our care well.

STANLEY

One night the phone rang. It was a lady who worked in as a teacher in the nearby town of Lee's Summit. She had a boy in her class who had been tearful most of the day. When she tried to console him, he just kept saying his grandfather was going to kill his dog.

The boy told the teacher that his dog, named Stanley, and a couple of the other dogs had been out in the yard to play. One of his grandfather's chickens had been killed, and his grandfather was sure Stanley had killed the chicken. He threatened to shoot Stanley with a shotgun if the boy did not find the dog a new home within 24 hours.

The boy told his teacher how afraid Stanley was of people, especially men, because his grandfather hated his dog and was not nice to it.

The teacher told me if I would come get Stanley from her house, she would go convince the grandfather to give him to her to keep him safe. She was traveling out by where the boy lived that evening after school to take her girls to a party and would be happy to bring Stanley to Lee's Summit where I could pick him up.

I told her I would be very happy to come get him.

When I got to her house she said, "He is a great dog but very afraid of men."

When I brought Stanley home he was not only afraid of men, but he was afraid of everything. He would not come near me. I had to trap him to get a leash on him to take him to the veterinarian to get his shots. I had to corral him to get him into the house at night to feed him. He must have had some very bad experiences for him not to trust people.

Stanley was a strikingly beautiful, young boy and was easily adoptable because of his looks, but I never thought anyone would take on a dog with that much distrust. Many people nowadays want a perfect dog, without work. In fact, many people think dogs like the ones in rescue should not have any issues at all since they are older dogs, not puppies. They automatically think they should be house-trained and not chew like they might have when they were teething. A lot of the dogs we get into Rescue have their own problems that have to be worked out and, sometimes it is not easy to do so.

I received a few applications for Stanley but only one seemed very promising--a young lady studying to be a veterinarian fell in love with his picture and wanted to adopt him.

We met with her and Stanley seemed to be okay. But she was about to get married, so she wanted to make sure her fiancé liked Stanley, as well. He was out of town when we met, so we arranged another meeting.

When I met the fiancé, I was not so sure. He was so aloof, saying he could train any dog to do as he wished. I just did not like his attitude and wasn't sure this was going to be the right home for Stanley, but they wanted to try and see how he would do in a new home so I let them take him to their house and see how he would do. The woman was as nice as she could be and her fiancé was very handsome and polite, but he just had an air about him that I did not think would make Stanley feel at home.

Boy, was I wrong! He and Stanley were best buddies. Stanley went everywhere with the man. Stanley started coming out of his shell and became a very friendly dog. I guess the fiancé knew what he was talking about. Maybe it was the kindness he had plus the confidence that made Stanley feel safe with him.

Whatever it was, it worked and Stanley found a great home.

STEWIE

Being a Rescue, I have seen a lot of sadness in my time, but this one shocked me so badly that I almost passed out. I took this poor boy from a local pound and he was in such bad shape I almost lost it when I went to pick him up.

It was five days from the time they first contacted me until I was able to bring him into rescue. He needed some medical attention, so on Thursday I told them I would take him. On

Friday, they took him to the veterinarian to get his vetting done for his heartworm shots and exam. On Saturday, they called me to say that the boy was in such bad shape, that the vet said he needed to be put down.

Thank goodness they did not listen to the vet, telling him that the dog was being taken into rescue. It was too late Saturday to get him vetted, so the vet treated him on Monday and released him Tuesday afternoon, when I brought him home.

His condition is so sad and unbelievable. He is almost bald from fleas; he is so thin, every bone shows. I can put my thumb on one side of his tummy area, my fingers across his back and can touch the other side of his tummy--he is that thin. His front teeth are all broken. It looks as if someone hit him in the mouth several times or he chewed through a metal chain or he had been eating rocks. I have never seen such bad teeth before and I have seen a lot of horrible mouths on puppy mill dogs. I gave him a bowl of kibble and after he was finished eating, I picked up pieces of teeth that broke off onto the floor around the bowl.

This boy needs a lot of help. Even his feet and legs are so twisted up in the front, that I do not know how he walks and gets anywhere, but he does. I am not even sure if an orthopedic surgeon could even fix them. I have never seen anything as bad. In addition, he tested positive for heartworm; so he needs a lot of rest. To top it off, he also has kennel cough, and infected eyes and ears.

He is, indeed, a very sickly boy.

I just want to comfort him and let him know he will be

loved here in rescue. He has probably never felt love before, but he will now. He is safe now, able to rest inside a cool room with plenty of food and water.

Stewie is eating small amounts several times a day, going to the bowls of dog food that I leave out all the time to take a nibble or two. And he has been pooping nicely—I have not seen any more tapeworms since the first day he arrived. He is also medications well and his healing is coming along.

Stewie has made himself to home, claiming one of the nine dog beds I have scattered throughout the house as his own. Before, he was just sleeping on the floor next to wherever I was so that I could touch him, but now he has found out the dog beds are more comfy.

However, if I leave the room and he wakes up and does not see me, he cries the most sorrowful cry I have ever heard in all of my born days. He is so loud, AROOOOHing and whining and crying till he sees me again.

He's only been here a few weeks, and already he is so afraid of losing his food slave.

VINNIE

Vinnie came to us as an owner-surrender. His mom, in her seventies, said that she had fallen and broken her wrists and she had to be admitted into the hospital. That wasn't really how she was injured, but she was a proud woman and her story was always to defend others.

Vinnie—not his real name at the time; he got his name from us—was dumped at her door one day. She took him in and he had become her close companion. He was a very mild tempered dog. The woman and her 50-year old son lived with many pets in a rural area. He was well over 500 pounds, a drug addict, constantly after her to give him money for drugs. When he broke her wrists, the mother decided to put the boy in a nursing home because he could not take care of himself much less Vinnie, even though he wanted to keep the dog. The mother decided that it was best to give Vinnie to rescue

Shortly afterward, the son succumbed to a heart attack. And, after the mom got out of the hospital, her daughter moved her to Washington where she would be able to take care of her mother. Vinnie's mom called to check up on her dog every now and then, and to thank us for taking good care of him for her.

Just a few short months after Vinnie came to live in rescue, we noticed his eyes were always red. I put him on eye drops a couple of times, but it would only clear up for a short while, and then Vinnie's eyes were inflamed again.

My vet said Vinnie needed eye surgery; he was the first dog we have had that needed entropian surgery. Since then, we have had three dogs who need the same type of surgery. Evidently, Basset Hounds are prone to turned in eyelids because of the way their eyes are formed and the mass of skin they sometimes have at the top of their heads. Bassets are full of wrinkles, and although it is so cute to see these wrinkly dogs waddling along, it sometimes creates more health problems for them.

We started a fund raiser online. Most of the contributors were Droolers. One Drooler in particular, whose husband is a surgeon, donated quite a bit to Vinnie's operation fund. Apparently, she had had a dog named Vinnie who also needed eye surgery. And, thus, Vinnie got his new name. We named him Vinnie in honor of Judith.

Vinnie was a big Basset; he weighed over 103 pounds. Yet, he was very popular at the Pet Expos. He was adopted once by a girl in nursing school, but would not eat right away. A number of the rescue dogs need to adjust to their new homes, so they tend to hold back from eating until they become more comfortable.

This young girl had been trying for two years to work things out in order to adopt Vinnie, and she finally was able to take him home. At first Vinnie would not eat, so she fed him fried hamburger so that he would eat. Most dogs are not used to such rich greasy food. Vinnie had diarrhea all over her new white rug.

The next day I got a panicky call from her that he needed taken back into rescue. Poor girl. She was just too inexperienced to have a dog, but Vinnie was glad to be back home.

A few years later, though, he did find a great home with another rescuer that volunteered for Ozark Mountain Basset Rescue. He has been the top dog there ever since.

Many dogs that come to rescue eventually find the perfect home and those that do not live in rescue forever. However, they do not know they are in a rescue as this is home to them.

They are never crated, never without food or water, and always have a dog door leading to yard with more than an acre to romp around in.

This is their little heaven. Their haven and home.

WESLEY

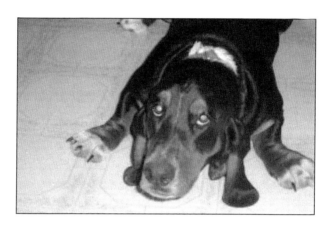

Wesley was a cute little guy. He was mostly black with the appearance of a bear cub, especially if you were looking at him from behind. When he scampered outside, his butt wiggled and he looked like a little bear cub bounding around the yard.

Wesley came from an owner surrender; they just could not keep him anymore. He would just duck and scamper butt wiggling the whole way and I wondered how anyone could give a cutie like him away. He was a young boy, under a year and he still had some baby teeth. You know what that means; he was a chewer.

Most bassets are chewers until they are two or three. They were bred to be hunters so they get more pleasure from chewing than most dogs. He was so cute and sweet, yet he was always getting grumbled at by the little old lady Bassets we had in our pack.

All kinds of dogs come into rescue, good ones, bad ones, cute ones, old ones, young ones. Sometimes you wish they could talk so you could really know their true story because all you really know is the story the previous owner gives you, and that is rarely the truth. No one is going to admit to beating, starving, kicking, or hitting their dog.

We got a leather chair as a gift from a friend. She had gotten it for a gift and did not want it. So, she asked Jim if he wanted it. The chair was real leather and had a vibrator in the back and heat!! Wow! And it looked new!! We took it and plugged it in. My husband got to enjoy it for about five minutes before we needed to go to bed, so we left it safe and sound in the living room. What a nice gift.

In the morning there was stuffing all over the house and where the nice leather chair once was stood a wooden frame. Not a speck of leather was left. Just a few staples and some white fuzz here and there and a motor with a chewed up cord. That was it; no more chair. And who do you think had a big piece of brown leather hanging from his dew flaps? None other than our dear, sweet Wesley.

A few days later, my husband and I were in our office/computer room--I am often working on the rescue budget and begging for money and he is playing games--when all of a sudden the lights went out and the computers went dead. I got up and went into the bathroom to get the flashlight so Jim could go downstairs to check the fuse box, but the lights flickered and then were back on again.

And then I saw Wesley half under our bed, with his feet stretched straight out stiff-legged and not moving. I yelled at my husband to come quick." I think Wesley chewed through the heater wire on our bed. I think he is dead what do we do?!?" Jim came running into the bedroom and touched Wesley's leg. He was as stiff as a board. Jim said, "I think he electrocuted himself. "Oh no! Such a sweet boy how could we have been so irresponsible as to let this happen!"

Jim reached down and, sure enough, there was the wire in Wesley's mouth. Jim pried it out and rolled Wesley over, but as soon as the wire was out of his mouth Wesley shot up off the floor like a bullet and ran out the door. He was stunned but not dead!! We were relieved but called the veterinarian and rushed him to the vet clinic to get a shot of lasix to keep him from filling up with fluid. The vet examined him. Wesley had a burn mark across his lips, but it was not bad. He was very lucky to still be alive. After that incident my husband renamed him Kilowatt.

About two weeks later I received an application from an older couple who wanted to adopt Wesley. Their application checked out. They were in their seventies, but were awesome dog owners. So, I took Wesley for a home visit. The people were very nice and invited us in to sit and talk. They had just bought a whole living room full of leather furniture costing them almost

$10,000. I told them about the chair, but they said, "We will watch him. He will be okay."

And he was.

Next time I was at my clinic the vet technician told me she was talking to an older lady and her son at her church two weeks after Wesley was adopted. The lady said how lovely her new dog, Wesley, is. How he is such a good boy and how happy she was that the rescue lady, Chris, let them adopt him.

It seems that before Wesley, she was afraid of every dog that her husband brought home. She stayed in the bedroom most of the time away from the other dogs. She was also bitten a number of times. She and her son told our vet tech that Wesley was the first dog they owned that she could actually take for a walk. She was quite frail and wobbly, but he was so gentle with her, walking beside her at a slow pace.

The son said Wesley was "the best gift anyone could have given my mom. She was very fond of that little dog."

I was so happy to hear that and that Wesley worked out for them.

WILBUR

Wilbur came to us one very snowy evening, just before the largest snow storm of the winter of 2004. He and his father were taken from their outside home because the owner would not allow them inside; they had no cover from the cold. It had been a blustery fall and a stormy winter. To keep warm, they would crouch together in the cold hoping to survive through each night and through the next day.

Wilbur's owner relinquished them to Rescue. They came to

us not housetrained--as outside only dogs—but that was permanently changed as soon as they walked through our door.

Wilbur stared at me with his bright eyes, wondering why I let him stay inside by the fire. He had not been warm like this since last summer when he and his dad ran the fields back at the farm all day long hunting for squirrels and rabbits, with the sun blazing down, baking their golden fur as they romped and played.

Now he was inside and warm. His dad just snuggled in, laid on a dog bed, and went to sleep just as if he knew this was where he belonged. But Wilbur, a little young and a little wild, jumped on the couch, then down, then up, then down again, sniffing around trying to figure out who these other dogs were and why they were all inside the house with the people. Not that he minded being inside with people talking to him and petting him. He was just nervous in this strange new environment.

It did not take too many days before Wilbur forgot the past and was content in this new situation. He had a home now, people actually paid attention to him, and he was being cared for. Such a sweet-natured dog. He had many, many applications for adoption because he was so darn cute, but he was never adopted because no matter how much we tried to train him, we just could not break him of marking inside the house.

Finally, just after the Pet Expo, Wilbur was adopted. His new family knew they would need to watch him carefully and train him not to mark in the house but they were up for the challenge. This family was a perfect match, with two young boys to play with. It was a great home in a nearby farming community, but right next to a new subdivision where the town had built a Country Club and golf course. Wilbur barked at all of the people walking by, so the neighbors in this new community started complaining of the barking.

Wilbur lost his forever home and was returned to rescue because of such a ridiculous reason. A block down the street from his former forever home people had cows; this had been a farming community for years. But, now, some people with more money than brains decided they just could not have a barking dog nearby; it might scare new home buyers away. So, Wilbur had to go. Wilbur's new family was crushed and it looked like Wilbur would be spending the rest of his life in Rescue.

A few months later, we got another adoption application for Wilbur from a lawyer, who, at first, seemed very nice. She lived in one of the most affluent neighborhoods near Kansas City, where I went to do a home visit with Wilbur in tow. We knew we would be returning home together after I explained how he still had a problem marking in the house.

When I got to their home I was afraid to take him inside. After all I did not want him to accidently make a mess on these peoples floor, but the lady asked us to come in and when I was reluctant she said, "Oh, don't be silly. Come bring him in." These people had a gorgeous greyhound they had rescued from the race track nearby and wanted a companion for her since her recent companion died. Not only did they have another dog, they also had five kids—four boys and a girl—the boys loved Wilbur.

Although the mom was a lawyer, she now stayed at home.

The father was also a lawyer. Both said they did not mind if Wilbur marked indoors. Their dog that just passed—she had kidney cancer—and they rationalized that if they worked through that, they could work through Wilbur's marking. It was evident that they wanted Wilbur and he wanted to stay with them.

Days later I called and asked how he was doing. They said he was doing just great. He had not marked in their home once. The boys adored him and he played ball with them every night. After years of trying to find him a good home, he finally found one.

This is one of the stories that make us continue to do rescue—finding the perfect home for a dog who was once unloved. That is what rescue is all about!!

Here is a picture of Wilbur at the Pet Expo.

He was in a fashion show modeling new gear for a dog boutique. He kept the costume on all day and never fussed once.

THE PBF AND ASTT

Two organizations associated with the Western Missouri Basset Rescue are the Anti-Squirrel Terrorism Team (ASTT) and the Pacific Basset Feet (PBF). Both were started via the Daily Drool, an internet mail list designed to entertain and inform Basset hounds and their people.

In 2010 Michelle Swartz, who is active in the military as an Air Force Medic, as is her husband, Todd, an Air Force Para-rescue man—both have worked within the Air Force Special Operations Command and in the AF Special Tactics community for many years—began a thread about Bassets guarding their homeland from terrorist squirrels. Michelle, posted that she "just kind of dreamed it up because her boys—Bassets Ruger and Colt—were so obsessed with the squirrels, they wanted to kill them—and they had slain a few. As a result, Michelle started the ASTT, the Anti Squirrel Terrorist Team, with Ruger and Colt as its founders.

Very soon after Michelle started her ASTT post updates, a couple of folks that have hounds that chase squirrels asked to join ASTT, with Ruger becoming the Director. Combining the Swartz's military experiences and the world focus on the 9/11 tragedy, plus the war against terrorism, the idea for the ASTT just grew— squirrels became an evil band of squirrelistan terrorists, Rats became RaTaliban, and Chipmonks became Chipmonsters.

Shortly after the ASTT was started, Val Brewer came up with the all-volunteer Pacific Basset Feet. She had written to the Drool asking how a Basset earned the title of prince and outlined her Basset Bo's dictatorial antics. She was informed that this position was awarded, not applied for. She then posted back that Bo had powerful ambitions. Both of her two hounds were born in naval housing at Pearl Harbor and Val had a human friend with the United States Pacific Fleet. These associations fueled Bo's ambitions and influenced his choices. He proudly appointed himself Commander-in-Chief of the Pacific Basset Feet (PBF).

Val put out a post on the Daily Drool requesting volunteers of those hounds that were not in the Order of the Evil Basset Empire (OEBE) (especially naughty Bassets who are more than one year old) or or Basset Angels being Extraordinary Sophisticated (BABES) (an exclusive Basset society) or who are designated as Princess's, Princes, Queens or Kings, and wanted to be a part of something. All bassets could apply and be awarded the titles and ranks of their choice. And, boy, did the volunteers come in! At last count there are over 200 volunteer hounds.

At this point, Michelle aligned the ASTT with the Pacific Basset Feet under the office of Boneland Security.

Debbie Winchester came up with a fink (dog talk for an idea) and thought of making bandana uniforms for the PBF and, as a fund-raiser for the Basset Rescues, selling them to those Droolers that are volunteer members and post on the Daily Drool. Val, an artist of cloth, who sews beautifully and is always making things and donating them to various rescues, including WMBR, jumped in and designed and made the first Uniform for show— and thus the PBF uniform was created. Val Brewer and Barbara Thulin sewed their fingers to the bone, with Val and Karen Metcalf promoting the uniforms—the uniforms are $10 each, very cute, and can be purchased through www.wmbri.org--filling the many orders that stated to come in. Everyone wanted to join and very soon almost every Basset in the world of Daily Drool Bassetdom was clothed in their PBF Uniforms.

Val kept on brainstorming. She asked her brother, Dick Brewer, to develop a Web site so that the Droolers could take pictures of their Bassets in their uniforms and have them posted them on the site. Each is a head shot, with the volunteer's name and title under it. The pictures are organized by Nancy Kay and are then posted by Dick on the PBF site at www.pacificbassetfeet.net. Michael Mooreland, a fellow Drooler, and his hound, Muldoon, awarded all the bassets ranks and, since he is a veteran, is the chief consultant on all things military. Each person who enters a picture states what their Bassets best talent is, and Michael assigns volunteer hounds PBF or ASTT jobs and ranks and places them in the proper division for the Feet.

As time when on, even more uniforms were ordered—everyone wanted to see their Bassets pictured posing proudly in their uniform, with their rank and specialty listed on the PBF site.

Now that we had so many pictures online of Bassets from all over the world, we needed to figure out something to do with these pictures to make the Feet more fun and to keep interest in the group.

Val and I talked about making a calendar, but there were already two or three calendars available to Droolers—one with Senior Hounds and the other Daily Drool Calendar; that was too much competition. Next we came up with the idea of placemats, but making them would be too costly. Val tried to figure out a way to keep the money coming into the rescue using the photos we had of all the Bassets in PBF uniforms. We both came up with the idea of greeting cards.

Michael had photos of tanks, helicopters, assault vehicles, medical ships, submarines, an USO stage, bunks, and a dining hall. He sent these to Dick, who photo-shopped all of the dogs' heads and bodies onto the ships, thus individualizing the cards. Everyone wanted to own cards with their Basset featured in his or her uniform. They were a best-seller and it was a big fundraiser for our Basset Rescue! Thus the Pacific Basset Feet Cards were born. These cards are the cutest things you ever saw and are still available for sale on our website at http://wmbri.org

The PBF is just a fun thing that took off like wildfire and just keeps building upon itself. Both the ASTT are PBF are just fun little, imaginary all-volunteer forces of hounds that give folks a break from all their daily drama.

RAINBOW BRIDGE

There is a poem by an unknown author about a place called Rainbow Bridge. In the poem, Rainbow Bridge is a place where animals wait after death for their humans to die so they can both enter heaven together.

The dogs that had a loving home are on one side of the bridge where they are restored to youth and playing and happy and healthy. Rescue dogs that did not find a home and lived out their life in rescue or dogs that never had a home with a person who loved them, wait sick, old, maimed and tired until a rescuer dies before they can cross the bridge.

The animals at Rainbow Bridge all have deep respect for the rescuer and all of the fine work they did here on earth.

The poem makes a lot of people sad and, I must admit, reading it always makes me cry.

I do not believe the poem is true. God has such a great love for all creation that there is no way He would let animals that have died continue to suffer.

All of us here on earth were put over the animals--God put them under our care. We are the ones who make a difference in their lives.

People decide whether a dog will be happy and healthy or sick and abused. We have that power given to us by our Supreme Sovereign. Rescuers are not special people. They are just people like everyone else reading this book who have helped a dog or any other animal find a better life.

Each person who has taken a dog from a shelter, or even a pet store, a backyard breeder, or a puppy mill has rescued that animal.

Sick and maimed animals, abused animals, lonely, scared animals are depending upon people to rescue their lives now here on earth. To make them happy healthy, well fed, and loved.

We can each have a part in that work now. You can start today. Take an animal into your life and you will find that you may rescue them, but they will in turn rescue you—by the joy they put in your heart.

ACKNOWLEDGMENTS

This book could not have been written without the help and encouragement I received from June J. McInerney, a self-published author and book reviewer, who made my stories more interesting through her superb editing skills. She took my plain words and molded them into a work of art.

Thank you, June.

ABOUT THE AUTHOR

Chris Bly grew up in the Midwest where the puppy mills and backyard breeders abound. A product of divorce with no siblings and a schizophrenic mother, she clung to her canine companion as her main source of love and confidence. Her dog never told her secrets. He never expected more than she could give. He never questioned her motives. He just gave unconditional devotion and support.

Drawn to her husband, Jim, who had a similar childhood and a passion for helping animals, they strove to do what they could do to help those furry creatures that could not help themselves.

Together, they formed Western Missouri Basset Rescue, Inc., and that is where the real story begins.

14844155R00061

Made in the USA
Charleston, SC
04 October 2012